This book belongs to

_ _ _ _ _ _ _ _ _ _ _ _

Dedicated to Imam Mahdi (ajtfs)

safeer tv

PIP'S FIRST FAST

written by
FAHMIDA HUSAIN

illustrated by
SEIF ALHASANI

When family and
friends get together

And open
their fast
with a lovely prayer

Pip learns
to trust
bit by bit

You've got
to remember
he is only
six

In summer, the days
are hot and long

Pip goes to school,
he has to be strong

And that's when he has
a tasty small munch

He fasts again from noon until dusk

Waiting until he can break his fast

He wants to fast do
like the gro...

Don't worry Pip,
you will very soon

The time for **breakfast** is almost near

Pip's belly is **rumbling**, can you hear?

HURRY UPPP PIP IS HUNGRY!

Then he gets ready
to go and pray

He makes a dua
for you and me

RAMADAN

This is a month
that is truly
blessed

Of all the months,
it is simply the best!

THE END

Printed in Great Britain
by Amazon

Pip is so excited that Ramadan is here. He wants to be just like the grown ups and fast all day – but can he do it?

Join him as he does his first fun fast this Holy month!

ISBN 9781720429975

900

9 781720 429975

www.safeertv.com